InterActions
small group series

Finding
Balance
in Your
Daily Life

GETTING
A GRIP

Interactions Small Group Series

Authenticity: Being Honest with God and Others
Character: Reclaiming Six Endangered Qualities
Commitment: Developing Deeper Devotion to Christ
Community: Building Relationships within God's Family
Essential Christianity: Practical Steps for Spiritual Growth
Fruit of the Spirit: Living the Supernatural Life
Getting a Grip: Finding Balance in Your Daily Life
Jesus: Seeing Him More Clearly
Lessons on Love: Building Deeper Relationships
Living in God's Power: Finding God's Strength for Life's Challenges
Love in Action: Experiencing the Joy of Serving
Marriage: Building Real Intimacy
Meeting God: Psalms for the Highs and Lows of Life
New Identity: Discovering Who You Are in Christ
Parenting: How to Raise Spiritually Healthy Kids
Prayer: Opening Your Heart to God
Reaching Out: Sharing God's Love Naturally
The Real Deal: Discover the Rewards of Authentic Relationships
Significance: Understanding God's Purpose for Your Life
Transformation: Letting God Change You from the Inside Out

InterActions
small group series

Finding
Balance
in Your
Daily Life

GETTING
A GRIP

BILL HYBELS
WITH KEVIN AND SHERRY HARNEY

■ ZONDERVAN®

WILLOW
Willow Creek Resources

ZONDERVAN.com/
AUTHORTRACKER
follow your favorite authors

ZONDERVAN®

Getting a Grip
Copyright © 1998 by Willow Creek Association

Requests for information should be addressed to:
Zondervan, *Grand Rapids, Michigan 49530*

ISBN 978-0-310-26605-1

All Scripture quotations, unless otherwise indicated, are taken from the *Holy Bible: New International Version*®. NIV®. Copyright © 1973, 1978, 1984 by International Bible Society. Used by permission of Zondervan. All rights reserved.

Internet addresses (websites, blogs, etc.) and telephone numbers printed in this book are offered as a resource to you. These are not intended in any way to be or imply an endorsement on the part of Zondervan, nor do we vouch for the content of these sites and numbers for the life of this book.

Interior design by Rick Devon and Michelle Espinoza

Printed in the United States of America

09 10 11 12 13 14 • 21 20 19 18 17 16 15 14 13 12

CONTENTS

GETTING A GRIP ON YOUR LIFE

THE BIG PICTURE

A mother stopped at her parents' home for just a few moments to pick something up. While she went into the house with her two little children, she left her car running in the driveway. As they were coming back out, her four-year-old boy ran to the car, opened the door, climbed in the driver's seat and accidentally hit the gearshift lever. He put the car into drive and it ran right through the garage door of her parents' house. The mother stood in stunned amazement as she watched the car crash through the door. There was *nothing she could do*. It was out of her control. Thankfully, no one was injured.

Not many days later the woman's husband was driving the same car. He was dropping off a friend at home and his four-year-old son was sitting in the backseat. As the father was driving up the driveway approaching his friend's garage, he realized that he was on glare ice. He put his foot on the brake but realized it wasn't going to do any good. As the car slid closer to the closed garage door, he said to his friend, "I think we're in big trouble." A moment later they crashed through the garage door.

His little boy in the backseat quietly said, "It's okay, Dad, the same thing happened to me last week."

I remember the father saying to me, "Bill, it is hard to describe how helpless I felt when I realized I was on ice and that there was nothing I could do to stop my car from crashing through my friend's garage door. It was a horrible feeling. I was utterly out of control."

11

A WIDE ANGLE VIEW

1 Describe in detail a time you experienced being out of control.

What feelings gripped your heart at that moment?

A BIBLICAL PORTRAIT

Read Genesis 1:1–27

2 How do you see God creating order out of chaos in the account of creation?

What do you learn about the character of God in this passage?

3 Genesis 1:26 says, "Then God said, 'Let us make man in our image, in our likeness, and let them rule over the fish of the sea and the birds of the air, over the livestock, over all the earth, and over all the creatures that move along the ground.'" If human beings are created in the image of God, and God is a God of order, what do you learn about humanity from this passage?

SHARPENING THE FOCUS

Read Snapshot "An Honest Look at Your Life"

AN HONEST LOOK AT YOUR LIFE

If you took an honest inventory of your life, you might have to admit that some things are not the way they should be. It is a rare experience to find a person who feels they have a good grip on every area of their life. Most of us struggle with feeling that parts of our life are out of control. If we portrayed our life on a pie graph and were to honestly plot each area, each of our diagrams would look different.

Look closely at a few examples of what some lives might look like:

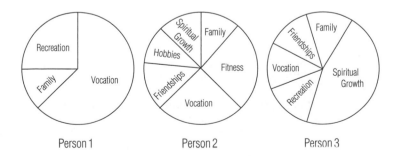

4 What observations can you make about the life of *one* of the people represented above?

5 Take a few minutes and create your own pie graph. Be sure it honestly reflects the levels of priority and commitment in your life. Think about where you are investing your time and energy at this time in your life. Some areas you might want to plot are: your vocation, family life, friendships, recreation, hobbies, spiritual growth, and commitment to developing physical health. Plot these and any other areas that are important to you.

What is one observation you can make about yourself by looking at your pie graph?

What surprises you as you look at this representation of your life?